In memory of John Sinfield
with deep thanks for all you did for me

Princess Pearl: A Royal Ballet
First published in 2012 by Hodder Children's Books
Princess Pearl: A Royal Ballet © Emma Thomson 2012

Hodder Children's Books, 338 Euston Road, London, NW1 3BH
Hodder Children's Books Australia, Level 17/207 Kent Street, Sydney, NSW 2000

A catalogue record of this book is available from the British Library.

ISBN 9781 444 90586 1

Printed in China

Hodder Children's Books is a division of Hachette Children's Books.
An Hachette UK Company.
www.hachette.co.uk

A division of Hachette Children's Books

Princess Pearl

A Royal Ballet

Emma Thomson

*P*EARL WAS SNOOZING IN THE SUMMER SUN.
The leaves rustled and birds sang,
lulling her to sleep. She spun and twisted,
wrapped up in her hammock, and suddenly
awoke to find herself in…

…the Underwater Kingdom! She was wearing a beautiful silk tutu.

"Welcome Princess Pearl," smiled Peridot, handing her some dainty pink ballet shoes. "The Prima Ballerinas are staying and they want us to audition for the Royal Chorus!"

"How exciting! I've always dreamed of being a ballet star," cried Pearl.

ROYAL CHORUS
AUDITION
TOMORROW AT 12 PM
Join and receive a rare pearl

Word travelled far beyond the Kingdom and soon more and more sea princesses arrived for the auditions too.

Pearl and her friends were busy getting ready when Princess Lyria from the Seaweed Kingdom suddenly burst in!

"I'm a wonderful dancer," she announced. "I'm the best at ballet and I always outshine everyone!"

Pearl was utterly speechless.

$\mathcal{A}$t the dress rehearsals, the princesses concentrated on their steps and turns – all except Lyria!

"Look – she's putting together her own routine," whispered Pearl to her friends. "We've no chance of getting a place."

Out of the corner of her eye, Pearl noticed a teeny-tiny princess from Shell Island quietly practising hard in the shadows.

There was just time for a quick costume change before the auditions started. Three elegant Prima Ballerinas floated single file into the empty auditorium.

"Would the first princess please take to the stage," called out a stern Prima Ballerina.

With butterflies in her tummy, Pearl leapt onto the stage followed by the other princesses. She danced with all her heart.

$\mathcal{A}$t the end of the auditions, Pearl hoped that her dream would be fulfilled. One by one the Prima Ballerinas announced their choices…

"Peridot!" She took a step forward and curtsied.

"Solarelle!" She tiptoed next to her friend.

"Pearl!" She pirouetted onto the stage.

Lyria's smile fell as the princesses collected their pearl prizes.

"*A*nd there was one princess who displayed talents we have never seen before. Her skills not only qualify her to dance with the chorus, but with the Prima Ballerinas forever… Princess Daphnella!"

Pearl couldn't believe her eyes – it wasn't Lyria but the tiny princess from Shell Island.

The Kingdom erupted into great cheers. Even Lyria couldn't help congratulating Daphnella.